VOLTA

an obscurity of poets

VOLTA

an obscurity of poets

edited by Sophie Essex

salò press

Aardvark • Anteater • Armadillo • Bandicoot • Coati Desman • Echidna • Elephant Shrew • Opossum Paddlefish • Pangolin • Pig-Nosed Turtle • Pinocchio Frog Platypus • Potoroo • Proboscis Monkey • Saiga Antelope Solenodon • Tamandua • Tapir • Tenrec

ISBN number: 978-0-9933508-8-7

Printed and Bound by 4Edge

Cover art by Becha
www.becha.me

Typeset by Andrew Hook

Published by:
Salò Press
85 Gertrude Road
Norwich
UK

editorsalòpress@gmail.com
www.salòpress.weebly.com

Table of Contents

Introduction: Sea Urchins in Bathwater

The work of a poet is the life of a poet, and vice versa

> - Tennessee Williams, *Suddenly, Last Summer*

Volta formed naturally out of my adoration for Norwich with its in & out of poets; transitory convergences that thrill, spark, foster positive emotion. Why wouldn't I want to share the gorgeousity of that with others?

I hope Volta both as space and object flaunts with the best intentions my love for the constant flux crush agitation of our city & its obscurities.

chaotically

Sophie, February 2018

JANUARY

Molly Pearson ~ xviii

if i were to write *i love you like paracetamol*
clings, residual to the weft of follicles
on my scalp, what will happen? you become
abandoned in my body like fragments of drug,
the bare orange night spreading forth &
back through blinds, the terror
of sitting here & trying to do this
again. there is in me this slab of connection,
uncooked need. it is not for you. there is
a pale expanse of touch slipping down
like a pill, an off-white moon
who picks her disconsolate, dislocate face
in the mirror. i want to put all your hair in
my mouth. i don't know how to write poetry

MOLLY PEARSON grew up in St Albans, Hertfordshire. She
is currently studying for an MA in Poetry at the University of
East Anglia. She was the 2016 receipient of the Ink, Sweat
& Tears Scholarship, and her work has most recently been
published by Ink, Sweat & Tears and Egg Box.

Kat Franceska ~ When Paint Flakes

Simon and Jessica are in the shower
, still. It has been fifteen years.
His hand now moulded to her cheek,
cold water runs along the ridges
between their skin.
This kiss cares not for dust gathering
on bottles or soap. The peach tub
is waiting for their bodies to drop,
let their knees crease. Feet cannot
prop up first love for much longer.

KAT FRANCESKA writes about the life model, the work of art, and the everyday. She has a BA (Hons) in Fine Art and is currently studying for an MA in Poetry. She finds classrooms uninspiring. She misses the studio.

Flo Reynolds ~ venus rising

tethered by black nylon
the ocean & its cumuli
are the proper negatives
pyloning away into mirror

tiny shadow i in a small shadow
following the balloon i fly in
whale on the end of a ribbon
i look on from above when

venus rises
aquatic kazoobirds hail her
night flowers & the flowers night
observatory sweat & flourish

FLO REYNOLDS' poems have appeared in *Magma, Fur-Lined Ghettos, Lighthouse* and *others.*

Russell J Turner ~ Locking Up Dancers

Lucia Anna Joyce. Trieste 1907. Northampton 1982.

Lucia stands stock still:
the clock ticks.
Her will is being tested here,
but she will not be bested here,
she has too much invested here
in a family still fighting with posterity –
mother, brother, father, lover;
a daughter treated like the other.

For I have seen her bite her lips
and comb her hair against the grain,
but not to launch a thousand ships,
and not to show the world she's sane,
and not to please the Dublin lad
who treats her like a calling card –
an appetiser for her dad,
a passport to some holy bard.

But oh Lucia, that was way too hard.
Like Icarus, if he survived
that final, fatal dive,
and no myth now, and still alive
to limp alone along some blinding beach,
shaking your sadness at the sun's mistake –
no longer dancing in the wake,
a shining girl, just out of reach.

For you have fallen far too far,
barbiturates and burning hands,
a biting wind, a single star,
a stranger to your father's land,
a stranger rapt within your skin –
analysis is all the rage,
with dancers locked up on a whim
from Trieste to an English cage.

But oh Lucia, that was just a stage
the world turned through, and you turned too,
but widdershins.

You plough your lovely, lonely furrow,
shake off the straitjacket of sorrow,
forget all memory of tomorrow –
this clockwise life, so full of strife,
doomed to be the unwed wife

who paints the walls of Plato's Cave
with fire from her father's pen,
to bind her body like a slave
and never, ever, dance again.
But I have seen her shake her hips
and shimmy through the Paris rain,
and I have seen her bite her lips
and comb her hair against the grain.

RUSSELL J TURNER is a poet, actor and broadcaster based in Norwich. He is founder of headCRASH spoken word and a member of the 28 Sonnets Later collective. He has been published in various print and online journals, performed at gigs and festivals across the country, and is currently working on his first live lit show, 'The Vodka Diaries'.

James Cooper ~ Lucy

There's a lot of dopamine running through my brain. I can see it in your wide eyes you're filled with much the same. You take my hand and pull me out into the middle of the floor, I warn you though I'm pretty un-coordinated, we'll probably fall. I'm not thinking about the arse I'm making of myself for once, I'm not thinking of what happens next or what happened before I'm not even thinking any more just moving and grooving and my anxieties losing then comes that hand back again now my brain you're confusing. The lights are there just for you, bouncing around finding beautiful ground to bounce from, creating a halo in the club throng around your beaming face. The song was written decades ago for this moment, every single time it's played just to practice for this, then we kiss and kiss and hundreds of people around vanish, we kiss and kiss and the music washes over me and the hands I'm holding yours with don't feel attached, we kiss and kiss and seconds later the lights come on. My feet are on the ground, my head in outer space, I can see how hard I'm tripping now and run to leave this place. I'll see you again but never that face, that smile shared in seconds unspared from actual participation doesn't mean anything between us, I don't feel for you, but in seconds shared in moments unspared I really fell in love with you.

JAMES COOPER is a young writer from Leicester, mainly writing on the themes of contemporary politics, love and mental health. They aim to bridge the gap between poetic techniques and rhythmical styles utilised in rap, to create spoken word which resembles aspects of both.

Charles Pritchard ~ Wetsuit

As though it were skin, but automatic, it
danced upon the ceiling from
  your hands,
    that were a wicker basket,
    turned like praxinoscopes, spliced and
      glowing from the centre.
higgs bosons scattered like chalkdust from a clap, telling
  each limb to drop from the plasterwalls and
perhaps you should get some sleep, i said,
     i asked what it meant
as the blinds snapped open (you brush the clavier of morning)
and you said it is taming silence, making it dance
to the elliptical childhood
  i woke from, counting scleral vessels
in my bathroom mirror. Those dreamless hours,
If we remember first fears
  of forms (their anatomies on the wall),
they fade, as dying penumbras, once apprehended,
  as we tear our thumbnails to each.

CHARLES PRITCHARD is a third year American and English Literature student at UEA originally from Manchester, currently on a study abroad year in Vermont.

Samantha Rajasingham ~ a soufflé (une bite)

a soufflé that never falls
never fails
beaten within seconds of collapse
folded in space
waltzing with indecent partners
even a gross roquefort
can provide wobbly excitement

a smooth tower
hiding a homogenous glop
one eyed solitude
a souffle, souille, sublime
a lingering sigh against time
blown up, grown up
emptied and infirm

a possibility built on hot air
gestating in the squalor
of rank and dirty ovens
full of hollow questions
a lump free faithfulness

all technique, smothered and smotherer
this catholic appetite
this chaste awakening
spoon gestating
an exquis
a fucking show off

a round moonface
no gash for some permission
your great mouthful
of so much whatever
delicious to behold
i never want to come

SAMANTHA RAJASINGHAM *has been a muse, amused, and has seen a moose. She lives in her head and in Norwich and has been on French television imitating cheese.*

Mide Sotubo ~ There & Back

I have just come back from adventures of land that was
   unknown to me
I gave you a year of my life basking in your symphony
And you showed me my reflection like never before

I have seen the highest of the high and lowest of the lows
But in between it all, I found a little piece of home
It wasn't all roses and jokes like they made it out to be
Albeit I didn't move that far
But away from home, is away from home
And it took being away from home to find a little piece of
   home wherever I went

I found and understood the true meaning of friendship
Never before has a ship sailed so close to home
That it docked right there in my chest
And now I struggle to let you leave

Dare I say, I found love
I have learned that I love deep and love cuts deep
When given the opportunity I am pretty darn good at love
   poems
Or quite the opposite when love is no longer on the table
Some love is only meant to be temporary, it seems
And I have learned that, that is okay

I have cried
Laughed some of my greatest and heartiest laughs
I wanted to quit, Lord knows I was so close
I stayed up dreaming of a life where poetry was all I ever did
And wishing Law could somehow go sue, I mean screw itself
And give me back the time I spent with my face between
   the pages
Of cases I'd never remember the names the of in a few days

I have experienced the effects of a city not so cultural
That my skin raises questions
And black face is part of a national holiday
I have explained my hair to more people than I care to
   remember
Repeated yes, I am indeed from London

When given sceptical looks
That translate into – where are you really from?

I have lived with people who could not see eye to eye with me
And seen privilege at it's finest
Pushed me out of my comfort zone
But showed me how to own my skin

I had the grace of performing to a people that were not
   my own
In a language that was not their own
But they welcomed me there and even welcomed me back
Like I was their own

So to urban woorden guys that gave me my first stage and
   a mic
To the band that we formed, The Backsitters – a mixture
of poetry, song and the sickest of instruments
We click like the dream girls behind James Early
It all started with that cover of Gnarls Barkley
To the language, that I have developed a love for
Although I'm still learning how to pronounce these Dutch
   words
I have some things down, most things are still   fuzzy
But I have got a hunger in my belly and a thirst for the
   flemish

You showed me who I was
And showed me who I wasn't
You tested my faith
And you tested these words
Damn how it feels to be away for a year
To come back like it never happened
To miss birthdays and weddings
But it was worth it in the end

Leuven you brought me to friends
I never knew I had
You see, we come for the city
But it's the people that make us stay
You gave me stages to share my heart on my sleeve
And ears that willingly listened to my heart bleed

You gave me home
Temporary though it was
But I have learnt that home is as far as you can take your
  happiness
And it followed me there and back.

MIDE SOTUBO, *a future lawyer and poet, has been writing poetry since age 10. Her work reflects lessons she has learned throughout her childhood and adult life, experiences with others and her own life experiences, her faith and the stories of others. As an advocate for anti-trafficking and anti-slavery, her poetry also shines a light on these issues and the fight for social justice.*

FEBRUARY

Rosie Quattromini ~ dream no 7 in collaboration with iphone

the only problem is the fact
the fact is that i have to go back
the fact is that you are not there
the fact is my wife is just a woman who can make a good point
the fact is that i can't remember what happened to her
what happened to my wife when she got home from the woods
the only way to get back is through the woods
the fact is that i can't believe that i have a wife
the fact is that i can do it for myself
the fact is that i am my own wife

the fact is that my wife died when she came back through the woods
the woods of the world are also the same as she
i asked for my wife to come and she came and she said she was just leaving
my wife is just leaving the house and i am going to kill her for the first time
i am going to kill her when she comes back through the woods
i am going to kill her many times but she doesn't even care
the fact is that i am my own wife
my wife died when she came back through the woods
of course i don't think i can be a wife
my wife came back through the woods and i was going to kill her
of course i don't think i can be a good wife

the fact is that i am my own wife
i heard it from my wife's personal friend
i am my own wife and she came back through the woods
i came back through the woods and i killed my own wife
my wife's personal friend is a small town in nebraska
my wife tells her everything
my wife died when she came back through the woods with me
i killed my wife when we came back through the woods together

the fact is that i am my own wife
the fact is that i am my own wife
the fact is that i am my only wife
i came back through the woods and i was thinking about
what she did when she was in the dark of
the world and i had to kill her for her own good
i died for my own wife
i died for my own good

*

the shape of everything is a triangle in the end
the vegetarian version of the world is so much better
i'm so tired of being able to sleep
the shape of the world is a good one
the shape of my body is just a bit weird
the shape of my body is not finished
the only shape is a triangle in the darkness
in the darkness the world will say that i am not working for
it
that i am not going where it had planned
but that is okay
i'm not going to sleep tonight so i'll let it come to the
darkness
the darkness says that you can make it through the world
and you will be a good person

*

my wife took herself through the triangle woods
she told me she was going to come home
she told me she was going to go to sleep now
she felt the shape of my body and i felt hers
the fact is that her body is my body
the fact is that i am my own wife
i walked through the woods of the world and i had not
planned it
but when i saw my wife i knew it was going to be okay
we are good people
we are vegetarians
my wife and i are good people and we have to go to sleep
now
we will go to sleep in the woods and we will rest
the triangle will keep us safe and we will be okay in the

darkness
the darkness is a triangle and this will stop me from killing
my wife
i had a dream where i killed my own wife in the woods
and the worst part is that i was my own wife

when my wife took a selfie i looked great
the fact is that i am my own wife
i sent my wife a selfie and she texted back
she said i looked cute and heart eyes emoji
i took a selfie in the woods and my face was a triangle
the shape of everything is a triangle in the end
in the end everything is in the dark woods
the woods of the world are a great place for selfies
the lighting is just right
my wife looks great in the lighting in the woods of the world
her face looks just like a triangle
she is very beautiful

together my wife and i can keep things safe
we will cook together and we will go to sleep together
we will have a dream about walking in the woods
my wife and i are very soft and gentle

*Abandoned in the forest as a child, **ROSIE QUATTROMINI** was raised by wolves. Her poetry has been published by Eggbox and Troposphere Editions, and she performs regularly and howls under the full moon in Norwich and London. She studied at Queens' College, Cambridge, and has an MA in Creative Writing from the University Of East Anglia.*

Alex Russell ~ i am going to paint Tim Burton's house hot pink in the dead of night

buddy
if you want to call yourself a writer
you've got to
you know
fucking write something

anything

why is it that frank ocean can take four years to release a
new album and everyone still loves him
but when i don't reply to a text for four weeks
i'm just some asshole
only kidding
i know why

i don't really know much about drake so i kind of made
things up about him and then believed them
i figure sometimes he drinks rooibos to try and seem like he
knows stuff about tea
and also because it seems like it could be the word
"rudebois" misspelt or pronounced weirdly
and sometimes he thinks to himself "heh, you're the real
strawberry rudeboi here drake"
as a little joke
i assume sometimes he licks the flavouring off one side of
a pringle and then like, puts it down
i don't know what he thinks we're gonna do with that pringle
now
eat the pringle or throw it away drake
christ

for some people, "write anything" is bad advice

i feel weird
i feel like if i was on a spacecraft alone for an extended
period of time i would start personifying the stars and
imagining the different friendships they would have
i feel like i would start to harbour fond feelings for them
based on these friendships and what i discover about their

personalities in how they interact in these friendships
but i don't think that i would assume they'd be my friends
at any point
i wonder what kind of mermaids they have in space

i wish this was a proper poem so that it could end properly
like, in a way that feels like it rounds the whole thing off or
calls back to something
but i'm not sure i believe in 'proper poems'
so i don't think it really matters
i figure if i end it with something i want to write
that's an ending enough, right?

if home is where your heart is
i live fucking everywhere

ALEX RUSSELL *writes things his dad wouldn't consider poetry, thought gammon was a fish until he was 17, once had Ainsley Harriet sign his Spider-Man boxers while he was still wearing them, loves you, and would be down to be penpals. alexrusselisok@gmail.com*

Olly Watson ~ Meeting The Dead Man

The room was musty cold, barbaric
and I thought the fella dead.
He looked at me as I stepped in,
"Sit down," the dead man said.
"Your name?" He asked in a tired tone,
with a face of peeling skin,
"Olly," I said, "and I'm from a little place,
and some chap has just brought me in."
"You know where you are?"
"No I'm not sure,"
and I saw annoyance in his eyes
"Jesus!"he said under his breath,
but he wasn't the cause this time.
It was a fella rushing home from work
to see his week old son,
who'd hit me as I crossed the road
out on an evening's run.

"You're dead," he said from behind the desk,
"Some fella ran you down,
and this is just a little interview
to confirm where you go now."
I didn't take it in at first,
the fact that I was dead
worried by the sickly tone
of the words he had just said.
"What do you mean where I go?
Is there still some doubt?
I know I ain't the religious type,
but what's this all about?
Is heaven getting picky now,
are the angels getting pissed,
cause Saint Peter is building shanty towns
and they're not on the list?
I'm not some bloody criminal,
though god knows I'm no saint,
but if there's doubt about where I'm going
then I need to make a complaint!"

"It's just the way it is," he said
"the way of modern man,
we get a lot of calls these days

it hasn't gone as it was planned.
Capacity is at its maximum,
we can't keep up the pace.
There's so many of you dying now
that we've just run out of space."

'Bugger', was all that came to mind
as I stood shivering at his desk,
"What now," I asked, and he replied,
"It's just a little test.
Do you believe in God?" he asked
"Of course I bloody do!
I'm standing in his guardhouse
being judged by a fool like you!"

"I meant when you were lower,
on the earth's volcanic crust.
Were you a God believer?
Did you give him all your trust?"

"Well, no! Of course I didn't,
but how was I to know?
Darwin made such sense
with his pigeon manifesto!
God was just a story
a tale we told ourselves
to fight away the growing fear
of those ringing death knoll bells!
And all that Jesus and the cross stuff
turning water into wine
was just a bit of banter
to help us pass the time.
No of course I didn't believe in God
no one did where I'm from,
cause we believed in science
the origin of man,
grew from out a cesspool
started with a bang!"

"You've failed the test," he said,
"I can't let you in!
it's too late to change your mind
and besides there's all that sin!"

And so as heaven barred its doors to me
I turned to look around,
and saw a sign saying 'welcome'
with an arrow pointing down.

Down I went the spiral stairs
cold and stony hard,
slipping on the rotted corpse
of a famous Stratford Bard.
And on reaching where they led me
to a room lit with roaring fire
I staggered when I saw him
for God had now retired!

"It's full up there," he said to me,
"Full of fucking pricks,
so I left it all to Peter
and those eleven other dicks.
There the ones who built it
bought the bloody land,
I always fancied a hammock
between two trees upon the sand.
Just me and a little ocean
coconuts to eat
a fire in the evenings
sandals on my feet.
But they said I needed kingdoms
walls and pearly gates
to keep out all the sinners
and all their burly mates.
But how do you judge a sinner?

It ain't as black and white
as some fella up a mountain
or forty days and nights.
They killed my only boy you know,
he was barely thirty three!
stuck him on a wooden cross
hammered nails into his feet.
And now they keep him hung on walls
in churches, houses, shopping malls
and pray to him for so much shit,
I'm not surprised he'd had enough of it.

He jumped from off the pearly gates
back in fifteen eighty eight,
and bugger me if I don't miss that kid
you'd never believe the things he did!"

God stopped talking then
looking back towards his fire,
and I was loathed to ask him any more
but I felt this unquenchable desire
to sit and offer him my time,
a bit of silent company
because he reminded me of my granddad
and I thought that's what he'd need.

I never did get into heaven
in fact I'm still sitting by that fire,
been sitting there for quite some time
but I haven't yet got tired.
But there is a thing or two I've picked up
sitting silently with God,
like to err is simply human
to forgive is a real job.
To love is just a piece of cake
to hate a waste of time
to live a full and wholesome life
the dirtiest of crimes.
Cause none of us is white
none of us are clean
and to set our sights so bloody high
is frankly quite obscene.
Better to aim lower,
try to be good more than bad,
try to make more people happy
and one or two less sad
try to be the sort of man who sits beside a flame
contented with its warmth
and happy to be out of the rain

OLLY WATSON is a Thatcher not a poet and isn't sure why he writes. Probably something to do with High Windows.

Minty Taylor ~ Tonight's The Night...

Tonight's the night that we make love,
Stop staring at sweet stars above,
Take off our hats and coats and gloves
And everything else to fuck.

                  And maybe you could suck?
No?
Okay.
We'll have plenty of fun anyway.
As long as I can actually find my way
in.
I love it when you start to grin
At my awkward fumbling around.

That's it.
Oh shit!
No keep going, that's it!
Harder,
Faster,
Wait!

                  I've got a stitch.
It's cool just give me a minute.

After, I dunno, twenty? we lie parallel,
I surely must have you under some spell!
You tell me *that's* the best you've had
And at first I suspect you're lying or mad

             But I guess I wasn't all that bad...

Now, again, we look at the stars
(Which are actually stickers that glow in the dark)
I take my hand off of your arse
And just stare.
Helpless,
And gormless,
I stare at your beauty.

MINTY TAYLOR is a performance poet, prose writer, musician, exhibitionist and aspiring sock model. He has been involved in the Words w/ Friends project on both volumes and plans to tour with them in July 2018. His favourite colour is yellow.

Christian Howes ~ And Then There Was You

I don't believe in love at first sight. But just to briefly clarify. I'm not saying for one second you aren't easy on the eye.

I'd parked up then walked in the dark up from my car, plugged through a half-mile mire of pub-pavement pile-ups to the one nice bar on parkside, when drawing near I'd rightly thought I spied a nervous-looking you, sat waiting patiently outside. And though it's true as you looked up, that primal sight set this quiet guy's tired eyes slightly alight, I wouldn't say right then that it was love... well, at least perhaps not quite.

A timid hug, and feeling bolder (relieved that though no one could call me tall, I was at least a little taller) we duck in out of the cold and order, tuck into our chosen corner, and we talk.

We talk like I have never talked before. In ways that people nowadays just don't talk anymore and soon it dawns that safely in from winter winds it hadn't been my whiskey or your effervescent gin that made us warmer but your wit and guile, your woven words, your wicked inner fire and efflorescent grin that bade me forward and before we know it, without the slightest hope to buckle on my armour, I'm soaking up your sentences as fast as you can form them. Basking in the heady scent of your effortless eloquence, barely caring if my two errant cents make the barest semblance of semi-sense. (Or at the very least hoping that you might just ignore them)

Because your mind's wistful missive manifests as music when you use it. And that, You blissful magic miss. That's what makes me adore you. As William so beautifully opined: "Love looks not with the eyes but with the Mind." And though our first midsummer night was of the slightly chilly kind, (plus I'm convinced I'd love you just as well if I were blind) I can't pretend it doesn't floor me every single time you smile.

So all that's left's for me to tell you though it slightly terrifies, and it's far too soon, and we're both a little burned and faintly fragile. Above all I just know somehow I love you, and hope it doesn't make you run a mile.

CHRISTIAN HOWES is an Irish poet and composer from Cambridgeshire. Writing since a young age his first poems were published when he was 14. A student of music and philosophy, whilst at The University of Surrey he was a member of the literature and slam poetry societies before going on to work as a Music Editor and composer in the film industry. He currently runs the online debating society Excursus Polemics and to date has had his music, Poetry and opinion pieces published by The BBC, Microsoft, Partisan Films, Patheos and Huffington Post. He wrote the score for the Partisan Films short "I Stood Up" Which won the London 48-Hour Film competition and he was nominated for A BAFTA for his soundtrack to the BBC documentary "Child".

Judith Howe ~ Drunk Poets

These streets are like wildfire
And boy, am I a pyromaniac
My feet pounding down the pavement like matches,
A lightness in my chest, for all of us
An absence of a weight that hangs over so many.
Just for this small brief moment
Let's wax lyric on the beauty of a bar
A cocktail, good conversation and maybe a cigarette at its
darkest.
Let's breathe the joy from one set of eyes to the next,
Let's forget the pages and pages still to do, and write
pages and pages of our own.
To be a stereotype of youth may be typical,
But it may also be weightless
When for so many of my friends not much is anymore.
So dance down this street with me as the streetlights blur,
And twinkle all the more because I'm blind as a bat and
not wearing my glasses.
In this haze, all I can see is the street and the night and
the smudged dots of the stars;
It looks a lot like happy.

JUDITH HOWE is a second year English lit student at UEA, Vice President of the Creative Writing Society and often found roaming the streets of Norwich looking to buy yet another leather jacket she doesn't need.

Sophie Bunce ~ Not my boyfriend just a boy friend

He's forgotten about me,
hasn't he?
It always seemed
like he wouldn't,
Strictly platonically,
We met on a friday
to study Economics,
We were acquaintances,
Then friends,
Then close enough
to tell the other that they sucked,
We got on so well,
He'd tell me to go to hell
and he'd laugh,
We'd laugh,
People thought we were going out,
Because i went back to his house
to look at graphs,
As we discussed speculative demand
people speculated about us,
It's laughable
For them to suggest
We'd be more than friends at all
He was a friend,
My friend,
But now I think
he's forgotten the girl
who he always made a cup of tea,
Now maybe he has another me
who is better at Economics,
Who likes Economics,
The thing is
it's harder to tell a friend
they need to lend
a hand
in this relationship,
Because he hasn't called,
And maybe i'm reading into it,
But he hasn't text in a while,
And i don't mean to sound lame,
But it used to make me smile

when he did,
When i saw his name
on my phone,
Lit,
I may have to say goodbye to a friend,
For no other reason than it just had to end,
People grow up,
Get on with their lives,
But a life with you isn't right,
Surely?
I thought you felt the same,
My odd brained
pal who likes Economics,
Though as the days pass since your last text,
I'm left feeling like some disregarded ex,
Your old friend,
Past tense,
Me,
Just me,
Sophie,
So I pick up my phone and I text you one word,
The obvious one
I don't want to say,
That rhymes with, I
don't want to say, that I
have to say,
Goodbye.

SOPHIE BUNCE is a second year English Literature with Creative Writing student at UEA. She is an aspiring writer whose family fail to understand why she'd want to be one, but encourage her nonetheless. She writes stories about people she knows, people she doesn't, and people she wants to.

Jake Reynolds ~ snatched & made true (from 'Dramatic Presentation of the Fireside Tradition')

The bird speaks:

> I am a good creature—made equal—have been fair
> with my plump rations—I vomit up my love each
> morning—good morning earth I have returned from
> a tricky dark—and my home has gone—if they
> wanted to make a statement—flaunt precision—
> burn pit beneath us—in the slash of cold air—
> where my spine is leverage—they could have just
> asked——over the way I hear the daily rituals—
> cousins I have never met are being wowed with
> bullets—over breakfast killers gush—gunsmoke
> is a comfort food—warm thing—indeed I am not
> one to complain—I will survive—I will in fact
> survive—my survival is just the ongoing accident
> of being seen—when seen I have just survived
> something or other—if they wanted breakfast I
> see mushrooms—meters down at the trunk base
> —just because my children were the potential ideal
> of Flying—does not mean I skitter over the word
> potential—Flying—and Cracking—Cracks Forming
> —my children—the ideal of Cracking Open—
> they existed in me as an unwrapped gift—they
> existed nowhere—but I gave nowhere a name—
> Cracking Open—and that is life—Cracking Open
> in a hot metal drum—that is not—it is the mirror
> trick—of a sustenance lie—built on the touchpoint
> of death—well how is this for defiance—watch
> me peck at a surly bough—watch me return my
> twigs to their rightful place—watch me settle back
> into my re-established home—the smell of being
> gone is all around me—it is surprisingly romantic
> —aka devastating—watch me watch smoke rise
> from the chimneys—o—people in your brick
> —what have you lost—what do you burn—you
> are losing your children to fire—I see the stains
> of their growing older—they burn things in
> private—just to reconnect with the heat—they
> are muted with what they have never known—

what you have not taught them—blind to the
consequences of flame—they tongue each other
in the dance—it is not what I want my children
to see—my Egg Crack Forming—I hope yours
wake easily—forgetting to blame you—but then
no child forgets—good—so here I go again—
good morning—watch my survival conscious as
my song—good morning planet earth—my voice
is now small—

*JAKE REYNOLDS is a recent graduate of UEA's Poetry MA.
In 2015 he was long-listed for the National Poetry
Competition. In 2016 he was awarded UEA's Malcolm
Bradbury Prize for his undergraduate dissertation. Recently,
Seam Editions published his creative-critical project 'Left
Alone'. He tweets @JakeAReynolds.*

Connor Enright ~ I can only hope

I've missed you,
your skin
beneath my fingertips,
your hips,
Lips pressed to mine.

And I know that now is not the time
to say I miss you,
but you're the reason to my rhyme.
And its only now I've realised,
that you're the tequila to my lime,
and now I am salty.
Bitter.

Sweet reminiscent vice,
rose-tinted beer goggles
on cold winter nights,
and strangers embraces,
hot but without the warmth,
hollow in comparison,
to an armful of bliss,
a rare kiss
that has yet to happen.

Yet if I happen upon a girl,
amongst lost souls in drinking holes,
Spit and Sawdust kind
eyes and calm heart,
short of breath and yet to start,
now is the time,
to introduce a new man,
new context,
no ex and all smiles.
No baggage, Air miles.
I can only hope
it won't take a while.

CONNOR ENRIGHT is from Manchester, and thinks Norwich is sunny. Connor loves horses. Connor once won an inflatable penguin in the only lottery he ever entered. Connor hates it when people bite ice lollies.

Jessica Rhodes ~ Flirting

If you turn on Tinder in the town you grew up in you can see all the boys you used to know asking for love like the deer that feed at the edges of the M1. You can pass through the county line like a ghost appearing only to the lonely & say things like, *hi I'm still here too sometimes*, or, *do you remember my mystery? it's almost all gone now.*

JESSICA RHODES *is a is a poet from the midlands currently studying on the MA in Creative Writing at UEA*

MARCH

Chris Beckett ~ *Extract from* 'The Lake'

Sounds came from the lake through the open window: croakings and patterings, plashes and reedy sighs. And behind those sounds, others, so faint as to be hardly sounds at all. Moans of pleasure, they seemed to be, or gasps, or muffled laughter.

For a long time, she lay there listening to the life beyond the walls of the house, and fighting the temptation to peer out. But finally a sudden loud splash was too much for her and she rushed to the window with a pounding heart, convinced that she would see her reckless shadow doing some awful thing like diving naked from the wooden jetty, with the whole lakeside watching, and maybe the gander in his waistcoat and his trilby hat, shouting out ribald encouragement. After all, didn't her shadow long more than anything else to feel the world against its naked skin?

But no, the jetty was empty and the water around it calm. The clouds had cleared and the lake was so smooth that it seemed not so much a body of water as a silver membrane, gossamer-thin, stretched out between two great hemispheres of stars.

"Are you alright there darling?" her husband murmured as she returned to bed.

She didn't answer him. In fact she hardly noticed him speak. She just lay down again and carried on listening to the night outside.

*

After another hour of wakefulness she jumped up again, having this time managed to convince herself that she could hear the creak and splash of a rowing boat out on the lake, and the careless shadow singing and joking in the bow, stripped naked to the waist, while its admiring companions – the fox perhaps, and the hare with his foppish beret – laughed and cheered as they pulled together at the oars.

But there was no boat, no shadow, no fox or hare, only a single swan drifting sleepily under the moon. Paired with its perfect reflection in the still water, it resembled a scorpion, a giant scorpion of the stars crossing some vast and empty tract of space.

"Come back. Come back to me," the professor's wife whispered as she returned to her tangled bed.

"Come back?" muttered her husband, half-waking once again. "Is that what you said, darling? But I'm already here, my dear! I'm right here beside you!"

CHRIS BECKETT is based in Cambridge. A former social worker and lecturer, he's published 6 novels including Dark Eden, *winner of the Arthur C. Clarke award 2012, and three short story collections. His first collection,* The Turing Test, *published in Norwich by Elastic Press, won the Edge Hill Short Fiction Award in 2009. 'The Lake' comes from his latest collection,* Spring Tide, *published in Jan 2018.*

Johnny Raspin ~ The Raggaskank

Many a night I meander through ghostly trees
Through a crooked wood that haunts my dreams
If I have to exist in such a place
A subconscious space that's riddled with fiends
I must stick to the well worn path
For if I veer into the dark
If I stray from which is marked
Something awful shall befall me
I must allow the creeping mist of fear
To summon the sobering effects of tears
For the trees wish to lead me
Their fingers evoke curiosity
They spell bind, mesmerise
My mind is being magnetised
Stop
Breath...
You know what hides behind the shifting tides
A graveyard of weaker minds
They were lead, so easily lead
The tune of this place infiltrated their heads
Under the beat of this melancholic tune
Under the beat that lead their feet
Away from the path that's lighted by the moon
Lies nothing but lies

This forest's keeper
Worse than any creeper
Devises ways to lure you deeper
And everything here works for his cause
The trees that lead me from the path
Into the clutching claws of the dark
The mist that brings fourth my sobering tears
Despises my manipulation of its fears
And how it serves to wash my eyes clear
But it will make amends for unintended deceit
What is that beneath my feet?
The mist has covered the ground so thickly

I can no longer walk so quickly
Through fear that I may lose my way
Perhaps the Raggaskank shall have its prey
Now imagine the thing that brought you most shame

And a thousand tongues spitting out blame
Forgiveness cannot hope to claim
When condemnation falls like rain
This is the place it wants you to remain
And once there you shall never awake

I must stand still and close my eyes
If I wish to leave this place alive
At this point straying would be so easy
The mist has covered the ground completely
The trees are trying that much harder to lead me
The the moon is too scared to send guiding rays
Into such a dark, insidious place
And I do not wish to stumble upon his lair
For I know that that is where
My deepest shame he shall lay bare
For I have seen a nightmare's nightmare!

Once I came upon a victim, when I strayed from the misty
    dreary path
The Raggaskank's handy work had laid waste this poor
    soul's body
He screamed of some unknown crime
That was committed in waking life
The mental anguish that he faced
Was multiplied within this place
But the damnation of my mind
Was not solely found within his cries
Instead, what I saw beneath his head
Was so very attentive to my dread
Midway down and around this poor man's neck an incision
    had been made
Blood trickled down onto the covered ground as I fearfully
    surveyed
Two crooked claws reached over his shoulders
The air and my blood at that moment felt colder
What sinister deed was about to befall
What treacherous torment was going to maul

This man?

This poor man who could barely stand
Was now in the grasp of the Raggaskank's hands
The beast rose up and was no longer hidden

He lifted his hand and with perfect precision
Sunk his claws into the incision
He looked at me with a look of derision
Nothing could stop his deathly decision
And within moments there was a division
The man was relinquished of his skin
I could see everything that laid within
The excavated man was tossed amongst the trees
Whose fingers would not allow the prospect of peace
But furthered, somehow furthered his gargling screams
Those shrieks endeavoured to fill my head
As the Raggaskank with his thunderous steps
Made his way towards me

Wake up wake up! I began to scream
Wake up wake up! From this detestable dream
I was to die, bedridden with sleep
Separated from reality
All I could do was squeeze my eyes closed
And shield my gaze as I fell to the ground
My prayers began to bravely oppose
The evil that hung in the air all around
When suddenly silence was sent or imposed
Upon the land of the Raggaskank
Where I had been lost but now I was found
In my bed, safe and sound

So when I fear the trees and the mist and the melancholic tune
And when I receive no light from the moon
To guide my walk through the Raggaskank's domain
I squeeze my eyes shut and I have yet to remain
But I wish to warn you, if you are found in that place
You must do as I do if you wish to awake

I do not know to what design my subconscious mind
    frequents that real
But I now seek heaven after walking in hell

JOHNNY RASPIN is a Norwich-born writer who studies English Literature with Creative Writing at the University of East Anglia (UEA) in England. Johnny is influenced by the likes of Edgar Allan Poe and H.P Lovecraft and enjoys writing supernatural, gothic short stories and poetry.

Annie Pence ~ A Camera Obscura

Looking out
Across the sprawling
Brutalist kingdom
Cut from concrete
Founding the fruits of our intellect
A shadowy mass
Appears in the tower of porcelain
Hanging over the dimming landscape
This man I know
He gazes
And I contemplate his loftiness
Soon, we all crowd round
Acquaintances and I
To ponder the intentions
Of this self, most forlorn
Yet, without a shudder or a shake
His flight is attempted
Icarus reels with reach
Wings unfurling with equanimity
Shadows shed
The sole travelling light
Brightens our skies
A sun of every measure
Erupting into waves of heat
His ashes scatter along the ether
Brimming with dusk
And out above us
Flies the creature
Flaunting fruition and flame
Up it ascends into Delphic depth
A limbo fashioned from stellar stagnation
An earthy existence extinguished evermore
And his lasting legacy
The ivory monolith
Standing
His camera obscura.

ANNIE PENCE is a strange soul, sensing surrealism in her sensual surroundings. She studies Philosophy at UEA, and holds a deep love for the Classics, Renaissance art, all things Dali and Lynchian, and puppies, of course.

Gboyega Odubanjo ~ A Great British Poem

You can tag this poem under the ebony section
tell it to take its hoodie down
ask it where it's from –
no, where's it really from?
You can arrest these words under suspicion
and ask why's its cadence so
where did it find the language that took it
from Bongo-Bongo land
leaving no trace of tribal masks or watermelon smiles.
You can warn this poem
once
that if it chooses to be abrasive
then we'll have no other option than to erase it
to rip out its tongue
spill concrete in between each jungled syllable
re-draw its lines
its name
and sing no songs and bear no silence
when it's gone.

GBOYEGA ODUBANJO is a British-Nigerian poet born and raised in East London. He is currently studying for an MA in Poetry at the University of East Anglia. He likes writing poems.

Mari Lavelle-Hill ~ The Art of Persuasion

Say something to make me
stay. I'm tired of chatting.
Converse me and make me
something immeasurable.
Tie each word to my body
like precious ribbons of
jubilant colours. Come here
and count the rungs in my
laddered tights. Count twice.
Check my bones aren't broken.
Check again. I know you
thought I was a nice girl
but my candle-wax skin
melts and moulds differently
when you say my name.
I'll knock you out your boots,
baby. I'll fold your socks
neater than the black and white
headline of the morning paper.

MARI LAVELLE-HILL is a third year English and Creative Writing student at UEA, originally from a small village in Sussex. Her poems range from sad to sexy and she has previously been published in HVTN and Octarine Magazines and in UEA's Creative Writing Anthology. Mari also reads at various venues around Norwich, including UEA Live and Volta.

Andrew Hook ~ *Extract from* People I Know Are Dead

I met the stool-pigeon watching the bangtails. He was a bit of a daisy and we bumped gums for a while before getting down to business. The pigeon was nervy out in the open and suggested a dive which looked more like a can house despite the canary doing the business with gusto on a low stage. Nearby a tomato with great gams drank tiger milk and in one corner some bums obviously out on the roof shot rats and mice for mazuma.

The pigeon was a weak-sister even to be peaching. He took a smell from the barrel but was hinky and twitchy as though he expected droppers at any moment. I told him to break it up or I'd take it on the heel and toe, but I was waiting for the Chinese angle. Then a guy broke in with a bean-shooter and the wild eye of a snow-bird. The pigeon was a wrong number, probably on the nut, and I was the patsy set for a fall.

I was in a jam, told the pigeon to climb up his thumb and then kissed him in the kisser to make sure. The dive lit up with Chicago lightning and the pigeon got zotzed. I pulled out my roscoe and hit the snow-bird across the button, smashing his beezer into his puss. Then the bracelets were on and he was bundled into the boiler, set to fry or gain some Nevada gas under glass.

Later I returned to the joint and chinned with the tomato who wasn't fussed I held a ticket. Before long we were drinking out of the same bottle until we were smoked and goofy and the number we came to was one.

ANDREW HOOK has had over 150 short stories published since 1994, plus several novels, novellas and collections. His most recent publication is his fifth short story collection, Human Maps (Eibonvale Press).

APRIL

Sara Said-Wardell ~ L-V--TH-N

I am looking at her head
through the largest telescope in the world
she: a main belt asteroid   or the sentient space ship
colossal woman   *finally*   dazed frothy at the mouth
& dead   dead   dead

I draw my map over barnacle / crater &
mark where I will cut her down the middle
exposing sky & steam   me: mortician   first man harpoon
hit -   she will fill the shape of black I make (through deeper
   black)
then the unprotected body buckling under all   space
but for now she floats

gurgling on her back like a baby

SARA SAID-WARDELL was born in London. She has a BA
in English with Creative Writing from the University of East
Anglia. Her poetry has most recently appeared in Milk: An
Anthology of Eroticism, and her chapbook, Reasons I Am
Uncomfortable, was published in 2016 by Egg Box
Publishing. She currently lives and writes in Norwich.

Doug Jones ~ from Posts

4/5/16

"Hall in refuge form, lit candles in vigil to incoming children,
many of whom built into a new arcade, skin perfect; native
roof. Villager cries an activity, tears across trestle tables,
into watercourse below – make offering to concrete up-
structures who dominate a wall, turn a massive art: forget
wandering history, keep the feet dry. Congregation settles.
One villager says, 'the hall's a sea, + I can't breathe'"

11/5/16

"Blackbird in heart of the church, builds out onion body of
her room – small numinous creature laid bare, she got a
soul, lost in stillness of desire – heartening her knit group
coat who imagined her a girl – her new cloth – built for
spring, + after that the autumn – fine square round a long
yard. A healing point, elite to regular change. In an elect
identity, fox moves through a garden – the same being"

19/5/16

"?What Fall, what chance of eternity without grace of
heaven – these Pills, Cuts – don't even tell me what they
are; had the blackbird head, legs – eye wrong. Said it were
the same as the yolk before, even when I comfortably
ate it. Oh how it made a squealing interrupt, supping at the
apex of a bud. Each bird turned out to be discrete – but
fixed in original sin; thus is my stair, my commit, to surgery"

*DOUG JONES was born in Romford and initially studied
English at Warwick, he then completed an MPhil on the poet
Bill Griffiths. While doing his MPhil he fell in with Bob
Cobbing's Writers Forum group – which was a huge
influence. After college, he worked as a nurse in east London
for many years and then as a doctor in Norfolk. He is
married with 2 children and is currently working as a GP in
Yarmouth. He has published two poetry books with Veer.
Work has also appeared in datableed, VLAK, Junction Box –
as well as a few other places.*

Helen Ivory ~ Wunderkammer with Escher Stairs and Cheshire Cat

Who paid the fiendish carpenter to build this house?
Who birthed the grinning cat that binds so closely to her
heel?
Each time she wakes, she climbs the ladder to the loft
in faith she'll find the maker there,
red-handed with saw, nails and midwife's apron.

But of course the ladder kinks off into another room
where the cat settles down to lap its milk,
and there's always a bottle there for her;
its drink me drink me label shrinks the day
and the cat shapes a cave from her sleeping bones.

HELEN IVORY is a poet and artist. Her fourth Bloodaxe collection is 'Waiting for Bluebeard' (2013) and she is currently working on 'The Anatomical Venus' which is due from Bloodaxe next year. She edits Ink Sweat & Tears and teaches for the WCN/UEA online creative writing programme. This poem was first published in 'Alice: Ekphrasis at the British Library', Joy Lane Publishing (2016).

Allen Ashley ~ All of These or None of These

All of these or none of these or sometimes in between?

BLACK

as night   as space
as coal   as a starless sky
as tar   as pitch
as ebony   as liquorice

Blackheart   Blackbeard   blackmail   black money
black diamond black pearl   black gold
black and white television   black and white stripes
It's there in black and white   black and tan   black and
                                                      red all over
is beautiful   is young and gifted   is the new...
The All Blacks   The Black Eagles   The Black Lions
lucky / unlucky black cat raven crow blackbird black bear
In the beginning before the Big Bang or the guiding hand
At entropy's end, the light and heat death of the universe
                                                      will be...
black ink   black shoes   black tie   black shirt
Whoa, Black Betty, bam-a-lam
skin   berry   currant   orchid
uniform   cloud
Monday   Friday   Sabbath
When black is brown and brown is black
the black corridor   none more   nevermore
Paint it black   the colour of cool and nihilism
little black dress   on the black market   battered
                                                      black and blue
black eye   black stockings and suspenders The Black Spot
black light   blackout
the monolith   black hole   black velvet
playing only the black keys   Black Ops   meninblack
burned black   black on the inside   vinyl   music
heart of despair   wall tunnel   Black Beauty
Back to black   pepper
the soldiers of the Black Watch
It's not a minstrel show

All of these or none of these or sometimes in between?

blacksmith   clubs and spades
black eyed beans   coffee pudding   tea
Out of the blue into the black   blackhead   black screen
potting the black   pot, kettle - not spoken of
black sails   in the red, in the black
black king queen knight bishop rook pawn square
Blaxploitation movie
black limo or black hearse   Black Boy Lane N15
bin bags   sacks   tyres   tiles   country
chess pieces   black lead
Blackalicious
friars   top mountain   berry way
lettering   matt black   glossy black

All of these or none of these or sometimes in between?

Black Uhuru   Ladysmith Black Mambazo   Black Moses
Fear of a Black Planet   The Woman in Black
The Northern Line
maybe once we all were black
the black economy   the hanging judge's black wig
black copper   Blackpool   black light
Blackburn   blacking the grate
A black man in the White House   Lives Matter
black humour   black comedy
Blackheath   Black Death
Black Books   blackout curtains
Jack   Frank   Roger   Cilla
nails scraped along the blackboard   mascara   kohl eyes
blackjack   The Black Library   widow spider
Black September.

ALLEN ASHLEY *is an award-winning editor and prize-winning poet. He is the sole judge for the annual British Fantasy Society Short Story Competition. He works as a creative writing tutor, with six groups currently running in north London. An earlier version of this poem appeared in print and online in 2015 in "Wordland 6: Black is the new Black" Edited by Terry Grimwood. www.allenashley.com*

Sarah Doyle ~ Kirn Dolly

I am the last of harvest,
limbs blonded brittle
by the late late sun.
I am hollow-boned
at All Hallows: reedy,

yellow-piped, stick-arms
flung cruciform open
in an embrace of gold.
I am stiff-skirted, wide
legged, fecund and

pregnant with home-
spun magic. I am
a threshing of seasons,
the safe-guarding of
plenty preserved in

my belly. I am all
the reaper's rewards,
cut from the final
sheaf, bundled and
twisted into promise.

Traditional English Dialect	*Standard*
Kirn	Corn

SARAH DOYLE is the Pre-Raphaelite Society's Poet-in-Residence, and is co-author (with Allen Ashley) of Dreaming Spheres: Poems of the Solar System (PS Publishing, 2014). She holds an MA in Creative Writing from Royal Holloway College, University of London, and has been published widely in magazines, journals and anthologies, and placed in numerous poetry competitions. Sarah has guested at many poetry readings in and around London, also curating events and performing as a jazz-poet in collaboration with musicians. This poem was first published in Samhain anthology, Three Drops Press, 2016 (Reprinted in Bedford Square 10 anthology, 2017; and in British Fantasy Society's FantasyCon 2017 souvenir book). More at www.sarahdoyle.co.uk

Cat Woodward ~ Sphinx

are you speaking with my mouth? are you speaking with my dirty mouth? sliding into me at a painful and necessary intersection, this is how we occupy the same point in space: i will kill you. not so recombinant but enduring community, when a boy who is a girl, a sphinxing boy, is always slipping off the eyeball, such a womanly blue boy and with redder hair like a dirty-talking sunset. like her i am picturesque isolationist terrorism. riddle me that. over here persons are lambent as anemones, persons sway in the dark stir of the sea erotically, light dark persons and we say abide with me. in your fairness and my stupidness abide, in that yellow dress, in that hateful shirt abide, abide in your working and in my not working, in your all-levelling colourlessness (and in mine) abide, lie and when you do so abide. there is a moistureless desert which abides, there is a petrified wood which abides, in them are houses suddenly abandoned, the planets pass over them and abide. summers of biding and abiding, for in the winter we die. so if to say cedar is to smell cedar, then what am i? if a bird is a snake and a lion is a girl then get your eye off my eye! keep that mouth away from me! you wear a face of quietly sad dislocation because you do and i am off-broken, drifting above vague, gloaming anemones because i am. when the voice that ends me calls it calls like i do, traumatised, needy, righteous and raging. the sphinx is the beast of peace i sent to devour you, with just your head left, sticking out.

CAT WOODWARD is a feminist lyric poet. Her PhD thesis is on lyric and robot voice. She was was born in the UK, 1990. Her first collection, Sphinx, was published by Salò Press in 2017.

MAY

Anna Percy ~ Void

I imagine that this is like being inside the song
blue velvet, dark as fifties crooners
Silencing as drinking ink,
flows in my nose and ears and mouth
not suddenly but with permission
I could crawl inside it and sleep soundly
dreamless, I imagine
its those nights dormicing in ripened corn dizzy and tipsy
drinking from the bowl sky
I can even put in the stars its lacking
it's given me that august Norfolk night
in jagged Manchester
drink it it in and you will see why

sometimes,

I can't breathe in this city
I have never felt so much myself
so much a part of all the world as there
no hustle just stalk sounds , owl and bat wing
you can almost hear things growing.

ANNA PERCY was born and educated in Norfolk, she has an MA in Creative Writing from University of Manchester. She has two full collections available from Flapjack Press and this poem was originally published in the first of these, "Livid Among The Ghostings". She is a founder member of Stirred Poetry a feminist collective in Manchester.

Adam Warne ~ Ash Road

when everything
how do people
through the night in the throat
of a grandfather clock
has shoved me down and is biting
returned home where
marmalade, oxo cubes, soft rain
stop crying it's someone's birthday
on the staircase are lost
in the loft the dun balloon
of a wasp nest deflating

ADAM WARNE is a research student at the University of
Roehampton and a graduate of the Creative Writing MA at
the University of East Anglia. His poems have been
published in various places including Zarf, And Other Poems,
HVTN, The Rialto, and Lighthouse.

Julia Webb ~ I have forgotten my password to you

I have made too many login attempts and you have locked
  me out.
When I request a password reset you say my username is
  invalid.
Someone else has tried to hack their way in or access my
  login.
My account has been locked because of too many failed
  attempts.
Some one or thing is trying to hack the admin.
You tell me to try again in 24 hours. This is a huge problem.
It would be helpful to know the location of the lockout
  threshold settings.
A locked account cannot be used until it is reset by an
  administrator.
There is no longer a default unlocking option.

*JULIA WEBB is one of the founding editors of Lighthouse.
She lives in Norwich where she works for Gatehouse Press
and as a creative writing tutor. Her first Collection "Bird
Sisters" - from which this poem is taken - was published by
Nine Arches Press in 2016. She is currently working on her
second collection which is due for publication in 2019.*

Liam Heitman-Rice ~ Long Unbroken Gaze
(triplet of poems)

1. magnolia

Is it envy, is it lust? I cannot really say,
But it's just what I feel, like every other day.
No-one else is at all aware of this pain I feel,
Or indeed its source,
But I assure it's very real, and strikes with tremendous force:

I see you both, holding hands, making plans
Really quite oblivious - -
What I don't grasp, what I fail to understand
Is why it need be so tedious.
Yes, we can see it plainly:
You are in love, quite beside yourselves;
Thank you for painting us this portrait;
I must say, you play your roles so well!
He the doting gentleman, strung on your every word:
Silent, nodding, smiling; oh, he's just enraptured!
Of all the boys you could choose, it was he that you be
  preferred;
You needed someone beautiful: tall, broad, of quite some
  stature
To compliment your pretty frame, offset by large breasts,
Which help us to believe you both are quite the pair.
As candidates for eugenics you really are the best:
Spotless skin, not too thin, bright blue eyes and pristine hair.
Radiant and colourful, you're both a single sun;
Blinding and unbearable, it's our attention that you've won.

    Hm.

Your display of happiness, well, it's rather bold:
Kind of twee, obvious, bearing little weight...
Not that it matters, if all truth be told,
Because of course you both are straight.
I suppose that I am jealous, I suppose I shouldn't care;
Don't they say in love and war that it's always fair?
So if that's the way it is, I guess then that's the way;
There's little I can do about it – and that's because I'm gay.

2.   departure longue

Dad hid the bong in the closet – I know he has, I can
smell it. Doesn't matter what you put in there, you can
always tell what it is. Shoes, food, books, booze: sooner or
later the smell comes out. Closets never hold anything
other than clothes, anyway, but for most people that's an
inconvenient truth; there's only a few of us who will
recognise that lies have a habit of seeping out, that they'll
leap into the light and as they stand there will shine all too
brightly. It is luminescence that can't be ignored and
neglected, the words that bear the inflection of their
undeniable reality – regardless of their undesirability. The
fact is, you can't keep something in a closet without it
eventually screaming to be let out, or just left to die inside
a dream that never saw fruition.
I ignore the smell, the sweet hot stench of Dad's hash, and
enter the room. I tap him on the shoulder with my eyes
and ask to take him outside. I've something to tell you,
something to say; for almost two years I've waited for this
day, to look at your face as I mouth the words you haven't
yet heard. Sure, I could have unveiled myself over an
email, written a message or a letter, but I don't believe
there is anything better than the physical contact of
speech shared between father and son, the open space
wherein you can react and respond.
We step out to the balcony and look down at the road, out
to the city, yet I don't feel much in the way of alacrity;
rather I am breathless, nervous, uncertain of what you'll
do or what you'll say. There's little else to be done, so I
announce myself with a start, the opening mark: with
"Dad…" I sense he's aware of what is about to be said, and
he doesn't look at me, he remains steadfast in his long
unbroken gaze elsewhere, staring at the blameless blue
sky that can't disappoint him with its Australian quality of
dependable banality. A reliable distant far-off insistent
straight horizon burned dry and brown by day upon day of
the same desiccating rays, fierce brutal and barbaric but
all-in-all quite convenient for it can be judged and
predicted.
      "I'm gay," I say.
      Staring at the sky, he says, "…yeah."
      And that's it, that all there is. Two years for a "yeah." I

bare my heart and soul and this what I'm left with, a yeah,
neither here nor there. A speechless deadness atop the
rattle and racket of the traffic below, and my father does
not look at me. He looks instead at the splinters of a
shattered closet, and I am free to go.

3. yarra

How strange it is; how queer, how blue
When I, alone, think of you - -
Sat at my desk, pen in hand, with one thought:
That of the love which you had brought
To me, for so short a time; a brief cut
From the intersection of our lives. But
It is a permanent fixture,
These feelings that comprise the mixture
Of joys and losses – it is *amour* that crosses
This abyss of skies blue and tides green
And of everything in between.
In lieu of you I have your words and letters:
These I treasure, but beside your touch nothing's better,
So alas we write, compose and think - -
It is the ink that gives form to what sits
Only in the heart and mind, seen in fits
And starts. It cannot be controlled, it's much too bold.
So sudden, who knows when it will come?
All I know, is that there is only one:
My boy, mein heir, mon homme - -
The young Australian, the one called Tom.

*LIAM HEITMAN-RICE was born in Western Australia and
moved to England in 2005, and turned twenty-one last
December. He is currently a second-year student of English
Literature With Creative Writing at UEA, and has had his
writing printed since the age of thirteen, in a variety of fields
such as school magazines and local papers. He was student
editor of his school's magazine in Devon,* The Courier, *and
currently has a regular column in the Norwich* Evening
News. *His ambition is ultimately to finish writing his novel
but, more realistically, he wishes to be a columnist for a
broadsheet paper such as* The Guardian *or* The (Sunday)
Times.

Fred Spoliar ~ Dream (for J.)

 Only, the city can be a garden.
Stretch out, I am speaking to you
    of the many houses of the vital night...
Late many strange make a masque
and clothed bodies turn only for us,
  for our sense of pine, borne honeysuckle, the hand gardens,
    we have put away guilt. Body, you map of air! over you
      strokes a fingertip...
Stretch out, tend to untethered sense of naming, play with
them in their beds, only elsewhere
is such as passed. Veridical dream in dream of peace,
    cornflower, hibiscus,
where we do not wake, dry press of articulated grass on
    bare feet, where is no
there is no unbearable second
where the concrete is. There is no waking,
but sessile fingers, leaves of air.

a) **FRED SPOLIAR** *is a London-born poet currently studying for a BA at the University of East Anglia. His poetry has been published in Edinburgh's* Inkwell *and* Crow's Nest *magazines, in* Oxford Review, *and has been displayed in the RSA as part of an ongoing collaboration with photographer Joseph Glover.*

OR

b) a **fred spoliar** *is a bad-folding human apparatus. smoky tall emits bad dancing and words. project conceived london 1992 now brought to east anglia has grown faulty and would cry.*

JUNE

Robert Shearman ~ *Extract from* The Dark Space In The House In The House In The Garden At The Centre Of The World

Let's get something straight, right from the outset, okay? I'm not angry with you. Mistakes were made on both sides. Mistakes, ha, arguably, I made just as many mistakes as you. Well, not quite as many, ha, but I accept I'm at least partly to blame. Okay? No, really, okay? Come on, take those looks off your faces. I'm never going to be angry with you. I promise. I have wasted so much of my life on anger. There are entire aeons full of it, I'm not even kidding. And it does nothing. It achieves nothing. Anger, it's a crock of shit.

Isn't it a beautiful day? One of my best. The sun's warm, but not too warm, you can feel it stroking at your skin, it's all over your bare bodies and so comforting, but without it causing any of that irritating sweaty stuff under the armpits. Though I do maintain that sweat's a useful thing. Look at the garden. Breathe it in. Tell me, be honest, how do you think it's coming on? See what I've done, I've been pruning the roses, training the clematis, I've been cutting back the privet hedges. Not bad. And just you wait until spring, the daffodils will be out by then, lovely.

No. Seriously. Relax. Relax, right now! I'm serious.

The apples were a mistake. Your mistake, my mistake, who's counting? My mistake was to set you a law without explaining why the law was being enforced, that's not a sound basis for any legal system. Of course you're going to rebel, right. And your mistake, that was eating a fruit in which I had chosen to house cancer. Well, I had to put it somewhere. You may have wondered about all those skin sores and why you've been coughing up blood and phlegm. Now you know. But don't worry, I'll fix it, see, you're cured. Poppa looks after you. As for the apples, good source of vitamin A, low in calories, you just wait til you puree them up and top them with sugar, oh God, do I love a good apple crumble. I'm not even kidding! Keep the apple with my blessing. As for the cancers, well, I'll just stick them in something else, don't worry, you'll never find them.

Give me a smile. We're all friends. Smile for me. Wider than that.

And so, are we good? Cindy, and what is it, Steve. I think we're good. The fruit is all yours to eat. The air is all yours to breathe, the flowers are all yours to smell. The beasts of the world, yours to name and pet and hunt and skin and fuck. We're good, but there is one last thing. Not a law, ha ha, I wouldn't call it a law, ha ha, no, okay, no, it's a law. Don't go into the forest. The forest that's at the heart of the garden, the garden at the centre of the world. The forest where the trees are so tall that they scratch the heavens, so dense that they drown out the light, where even the birds that settle on the branches come out stained with black. What, why, because I said so. What? Oh. Yes, fair point. Because at the centre of the forest there stands a house, and the house is old, and the house is haunted.

Okay.

Okay. I'll be off then. Night, night, sleep tight. Don't let the bedbugs bite.

ROBERT SHEARMAN is the Winner of the World Fantasy Award, the Shirley Jackson Award, the Edge Hill Readers Prize, three British Fantasy Awards, the Sunday Times Playwriting Award, the World Drama Trust Award and Two Sony Awards. He is best known for his work on Doctor Who, bringing back the Daleks for the BAFTA winning first series in an episode nominated for a Hugo Award

Mayura Uthayakumaran ~ Brown Girls Prosper

Vibrations of knowledge, wisdom and beauty pulse through
    every step we take,
Nourishing the grounds with stories to tell, talents to
    explore, love to harbour,
Pushing for growth within each other,
Within ourselves.
Building a ladder of support systems in a world that wants
    to see us fall on the first step,

In a world that shackles each of our hands under chains of
    'race' and 'gender',
D r a g g i n g our bodies to the ground,
Scrubbing at our skin,
Erasing us off the colour we were born with.
'*Didn't you hear*?' the media yells at the start of every
    generations lessons,
'*The lighter, the whiter, the better.*'

Yet the teacher is the one to wear bindis for '*fashion*',
Multiculturalism and integration is key, but appropriation
    is not,
Morphing South Asian girls into prisoners of our own bodies,
As our skin hangs limp on bones and flesh,
Following the manual of '*how to hide your culture.*'

The rejection suffocates us in the early years,
As the words of our mother tongue sours with the bitterness
    of blood,
Drawn from the crunch of chewing glass on every word,
Each shard digging deeper into every pronunciation,
Muffling and eating at the words of our language till we
    recognise it no more.

Yet we persevere.
We adapt, we evolve and prosper.
Brown girls have been prospering since birth,
Rising from the richness of the Earth,
Building it from the ground up.

It is true history has not been kind to us,
Yet oppression is *not* the only aspect of our past.

Do not forget the arts and culture that floods our heritage.
Do not forget the teachers, the scientists, the doctors and
  physicians,
To the activists, the artists, the parents and historians,
Guiding the path for the rest of us.
Urging us to carry the flame forward,
Challenging the '*norms*' written by someone else in history.

The first steps taken towards self-love and acceptance is like
breathing fresh air for the first time,
It is the feeling of air filling your lungs in a newly
  appreciated body,
Reversing *years* of integrated racism and self-hatred,
Realising *brown is beautiful*,
Knowing that the words we have to say, ideas we have to
  share, intelligence we have to explore *is* worthy and valid.

The extension of sisterhood is a source of never-ending love
  flowing from our hands,
The raging river perseveres despite the many boulders
  lodged in place against it,
Essential to the growth and nourishment of the Earth,
  barred by the manmade dam.
Despite the attempts to separate the river, it always finds its
  way back, to flow as one.

The magic and talent we harbour glows from within our
  spirits,
As bravery laces every word we speak,
Our backs thick with the resilience of our ancestors who
  guided us here,
Ensuring our successes are not anomalies.

Brown girls do not just bleed from every punch at the glass
  ceiling,
We adapt as individuals.
We elevate each other.
We persevere together.

Brown girls have been prospering since the beginning of our
  time,
And *that* is no surprise.

MAYURA UTHAYAKUMARAN is a second year English Literature with Creative Writing student. She tends to write poetry focusing on identity, race and gender. Her most recent work involves showcasing my poetry on the British Asian experience in the 2017 Ampersand Exhibition in Norwich. More of her work can be found on her website (www.mayurau.com) and social media accounts.

Nick Broughton ~ The Bibliomancer's Daughter

My father was a magician. Not a stage conjuror or a clown squirting water from a plastic flower at laughing kids. No, sadly not. His magic was brought from the reverse side of the rainbow, where the colours bleed into each other creating an arc of murk and ambivalence.

On the morning of my 21st birthday when I received the letter, I'd not seen dad for ten years. The court informed me that he was considered deceased and no longer a missing person.

He always made dramatic exits from and entrances on my life; forever on the move and restless in his skin. I remember him striding at sliding doors in libraries or supermarkets, making irritable gestures to wave them open. Like an imperial Caesar stepping on to Britain's shore, fanning away fog and the whispers of druids.

His mentor at university was Aubrey Scrivener, a writer and critic who also skimmed pebbles across the surface of the occult. I think dad picked up most of his bad habits from Aubrey: fearlessly rude, drunk, inconstant in love and perpetually distracted.

The final straw for me, for mum, was when he tried to 'initiate' me on my eleventh birthday with peyote. The aim, he said, was to astrally travel to Mars. I thought we were going to the zoo, somehow hearing 'astrally' and 'Mars as 'lemurs'.

A mystery of language lays at the heart of his final misadventure. The last entry in his diary, eventually returned to me by police, are the words 'Leipzig', 'peacock' and 'Ruby'. An arrow points from them to one end of a doodled rainbow at the top of the page. I have no idea what this cryptography means. A message in a bottle? A telegram to friends or acquaintances unseen? And does it matter much? The only clue I have to give his last words is that he practiced bibliomancy – the art of divination practiced by flicking through a book's pages and selecting words at random.

So, on my 21st birthday - the day that I picked up the key to the door from where the rest of my life snakes forward - I finally accepted that dad had found the portal which he was searching for. You see, another of his eccentricities was to obsessively pass under any stone archway – in medieval passages, ruined walls and church buildings – a rare look of hope on his face. And the only record I have of that face is in a photo mum took of us when I was five. In the picture I am smiling and his face is untouched by corruption. Behind us hangs a large print of the sun balanced above the moon.

NICK BROUGHTON *is from Dorset and has been killing time in Norwich for nearly 30 years.* The Bibliomancer's Daughter *is dedicated first to his daughter, Althea Angel Broughton-Squire and secondly to Durdle Dor, a stone archway on the Dorset coastline.*

Piers Harrison-Reid ~ (9/7/15) 'You Were 26 Months'

You were 26 months
I was 22 years

Your veins:
skeletal, leaf like,
splayed under your transparent skin-
Iridescent, almost.
Marbling.
Like faults in ice.

Cyanosing, pale,
Tubes burrowed into your bones.
Found in a bed of brown vomit; alone for 2 hours.
We weren't quick enough.
Nose bleeding from our heavy handed lack of letting go.

6 hits of adrenaline
Asynchronistic CPR
We couldn't make a difference to your ph.

You left at 17.04.

It was raining and the lights were too bright.
You sat like a king on the bed,
Your powder blue palms and soles glittering
As gold in moonlight.

And your dad's eyes cracked behind pursed lips.
As your stillness stung the air around you and moved
through glistening corridors.
Unannounced.

Until it withered and the corridors were empty and airless.

Still, despite the fans.
Still, as your mother howled herself desolate,
Into fragments then.
Still herself as it overtook her.
Still as the silent shuddering tears of the team broke
through the restraining emptiness before being swallowed
again.

Your dad thanked us.
After weeping into you.
Through broken voice.
Through his calm pride and restraint.

And grown men and women fell apart.

Your bedsheets were stained brown and red
Your skin was cold.

We unscrewed the tubes buried in your bones.
We took blood from your heart, liquid from your spine,
photos and hair and flashbulb memories.
My only regret is that I never saw the warm light in your
eyes.
Babbling and bubbling stream-like in the sunshine.
My only regret is that I never saw you breathe.

We will miss you, sir.
Until our eyelids close
And we too become a network of interlinked leaves
Waiting for spring.

PIERS HARRISON-REID is a Norwich based Accident and Emergency Nurse, and a far too occasional performance poet. Inspired by hip-hop, Slam, and Punk culture, his self-reflective and cathartic poems now tell the stories of life, love and loss of both himself and the people he meets in hospital.

OCTOBER

Julia Rose Lewis ~ Breathing Underwater II

The skin thinks. Slippery the skin and briar lie the brain.
Beak equidistant from each of its tentacles because it is
easier to imagine than a mouth at the center of its arms.
Than a moment in a man's arms. I see you as an octopus,
only, turned upside down. Head to chest to hydrocodone-
cephalopod hybrid makes me want to wash my hair. If
and only if how are you means tell me you are here. Dear
laboratory partner for invertebrate zoology where are you
means I want you beside me. Octopoda cradle.

*JULIA ROSE LEWIS is the author of Phenomenology of the
Feral (Knives Forks and Spoons 2017, from which this poem
is taken) and co-author of Strays with James Miller
(Haverthorn 2017). She won the 2017 Pitch Viper Prize and
her shortbook How to Hypnotize a Lobster is forthcoming
with Fathom.*

Billy Pilgrim ~ Guinea Pigs

Did anybody ever tell you that guinea pigs must be kept in twos? Apparently, if one of them dies, you'll have to buy another, or the second one just dies as well. Of loneliness. In Finland or Norway or one of the Scandinavian countries, it's illegal to have just one guinea pig. I don't know what the Danish Police do if they catch you with a singular pig. Perhaps make you live forever, on your own in a cage.

So anyway, because of this law, they have these companies in Sweden that rent guinea pigs out, so when one of the two that you originally bought dies, you can borrow a friend to accompany your pig right through to the end, until it dies of natural causes. That way you don't get caught in this endless cycle of guinea pig replacement. And nobody needs to die of loneliness or a broken heart.

If I were a guinea pig, I'm not sure I would want a friend rented out for me. Would you ever really believe that they cared about you for real? Or would it always be in the back of your mind that a direct debit was the only reason they stayed. I wouldn't want to share my carrots or hay, or toy that is shaped like a corn on the cob with some phoney.

But that's just it, what are our other options? When the one person that loves us, dies, and that we love, dies. Just dead, then what? Nobody else is going to come along and make us smile or breakfast. Maybe we should just let these poor pigs die. Because without their roommate they aren't truly happy and let's not assume them to be fickle just because they can't control their appetites

And why is our choice to decide which of these people get to live and to die?

BILLY PILGRIM is a spoken word poet with a plethora of experience performing to a variety of audiences throughout East Anglia and further afield, His work is grounded in abstract narratives which explore the reality of modern life. Often outspoken, always irreverent, this poet will leave you questioning accepted truths.

Andrea Holland ~ Post-Twitter Blues

Artifice acquired/ For its own sake is war - Hayden Curreth

What can I expect, how do I manage expectation?
What is there to get from this distance, from here
where years have come between me and those
for whom cynicism is as easy as a duvet or wooly tights
with sharp patterns that clever girls wear under bright shorts.
They'd put rumble strips down on school playgrounds.
Cynic, it's pulling back the wizard's curtain while at the same
  time
hearting lines in songs, the tone of the poems I see
sentimental as hymns: *oh rugged tree*, this is me
as St. Sebastian, this is me as love-lorn bitch, this is me
picking blackberries, not from the bramble, but out of
the fridge, first thing in the morning when my eyes hurt
and nobody is looking. *There is a green hill far away
outside a city wall*...but hey, screw narrative, my ire
trumps your scene. Look at me, look at me! I am
a collage of everyone's neediness, and form is as relevant
as restless-leg syndrome...lady at your laptop, sticker-free,
tell me what did you expect to see?

ANDREA HOLLAND *is a Lecturer in Creative Writing at the University of East Anglia. Her collection of poems,* Broadcasting *(Gatehouse Press, 2013) was the winner of the 2012 Norfolk Commission for Poetry. Her first collection* Borrowed, *was published by Smith/Doorstop in 2007. She has poems in MsLexia, The Rialto, The North and other literary journals as well as online. She has also collaborated with visual artists on a number of commissioned projects. Andrea resides in Norwich with her family, after studying and teaching in the USA for a number of years.* www.andreacholland.co.uk

Lois Arcari ~ Only Their Boots Change

They come and go as all barrage of insults do. Not premeditated, marinated – your words live like bees, diving and dying for their fatal sting. Aiming for bare arms and flicking through unwashed car windows. Our breath does not detain them. Triggered as they always are by the honey of bad drivers. At this moment they sting against the radio.

He's a – an – as if we didn't know.

As if the laundry list escaped our notice the last time. As if she's not got her hands over her ears trying not to hear it. This sermon has been strung along down every mile, each twist of road. But to you, it makes a shred of difference. Serves as balm to the aches and pains.

The everyday.

This is your justice.

Words that die with the dignity of flies and always seem to rot the air around us.

You've played at hunting him already, of course. 'In the army; of a sorts. So, you tell the suits, smiling in yours, that they can't expect you not to go for blood. They wrestle with their ball point pens, wishing you weren't such a hassle. There's been no true shots fired, at first. And you look frail enough to be ignored. But you made your start with a hundred screens.

That face pale in the glares. You'll get there. Like by like. Share by Share.

Step by step, and soon enough, you'll play God and squish the blot beneath your fingers. *Wanton, wicked boy he was*.

So of course, there are knocks on the door. One. Two. Three. Just like you've heard before. Like you've learnt to smell the swill of people plodding into telling other how to live their lives.

Only their boots ever seem to change.

Their steps sounded the same when you bobbed two big fat boulder heads under the water. Their knocks register at familiar decibels, ones brought forth by *neighbourly concerns*. The world. S'gone fucking mad – but that's how it was made.

Little toad sniffled out something too loud and now they're all on his side. Eyes wide rimmed with remorse till they're plucked par for the course in time. They're on the side of evil now. *Again*. Too easy to believe, but you still shudder. Keep your words in tune. Floss out the venom with an open smile and easy laughter. Even asking them for tea. *You know the cups will curdle*. Some parts of your true vocabulary still flit out, buzzing round the rotten fruit of the big fat mouth that called them.

The uniforms just mean they move slightly more stealthily.

Under your breath and everyone else's you mutter – how laughable and obvious that they'd move to protect him, him, the x y z a b c d bastard. *Cunt. Coward*. Criminal. And all those credentials questioned. In all your murmuring, you never check the faces of the officers. Their sheer resplendent boredom. Your wife smoothing down tea stains with bloody murder. The cat sitting fat and royal, defying everything, licking its arse at the end of the world.

LOIS ARCARI is a second year undergraduate studying Literature and Creative Writing at UEA. She has written for publications like Concrete, Buzz Magazine and the Tab. She enjoys illustration, bad movies, and hurtling towards the questionable with incontestable enthusiasm. She is no longer allowed near fruit bowls at parties.

Cai Draper ~ Millennial

Chicken pox dots round my belly button
Falling off the bike onto my forehead pissed
New Zealand garden, chainsaw to the leg
Burns on my arms from when I was a chef

In the scheme of things, they're rudimental
Some of them bad, some of them less so
There's a girl in my class who cuts her hands
Those won't be her only scars

CAI DRAPER is a poet from south-east London. He tries to be funny and poignant at the same time. He is working towards an MA in creative writing from UEA and would like to thank Norwich for being so welcoming.

Milly Green ~ *Extract from* Something Strange

The Darkness fell easily on the deserted lake. The moon hung above the tips of the fragrant pines trees, a glowing white bauble among the velvety blackness of the night sky. It was reflected in the shimmering inky surface of the lake as it lapped gently on the muddy bank before being dragged away from it like a disobedient child. There had been recent rainfall; the ground was slippery under the deceiving soft blanket of the jade grass and the air was alive with its smell. Flowers that had cowered prettily under the comfort of the trees like ladies under their parasols were now stretched out like sun worshippers, raindrops still clinging to their jewelled petals. The trees stood stoically as nothing around them seemed to stir, the quiet holding them all in its spell. It was like the place was holding its breath, waiting for something that they could not explain but they knew was coming.

There was a rustling as a fox moved through the trees, his nose close to the ground. He sniffed at the ground and his nose wrinkled at the strange sense of anticipation that hung in the air like the last mist of the rain. His tail twitched as a pattering suddenly rang out in the silence, steadily approaching the spot by the lake and he raised his head and ran when two small figures came into view. Two sets of footsteps hurried as they ran towards the lake, dew-soaked slippers sliding about on the muddy ground in their haste and one of the two had to grab at the other to stop herself from slipping. This nearly caused her to drop the large silver saucepan she was carrying in both arms, her small hands not even touching as the pan nearly dwarfed her.

"Careful!" An annoyed young voice spat out into the night, banishing any silence still remaining for good as she forced her sister away and nearly sent her sprawling to the ground. "You nearly made me drop it! Mum'll kill me if I dent her best pan!"

MILLY GREEN is a history student at the University of East Anglia who originally comes from Hertfordshire. She loves to write in her spare time and when not writing, is usually walking around with her nose in a book. She acts as the house mother in her home that she shares with a fellow house dad, a grumpy teenager and a demoted houseplant. Her boyfriend occasionally drops by to keep her sane.

Westley Barnes ~ Persephone

When you die
People you will have never met
will give your family condolences

When you die
Spurned former lovers will
send delicate flowers

When you die
People will be summoned to
make you look beautiful

The way that you felt on nights
you enjoyed being yourself the most

When you die
Cautious children will cry
without ever learning
of your conflicting views on children

When you die
They might hang the church wall
with pictures of weddings
and graduations

When you die
You may not be alone

When you die
You might be the first and
the others will all follow

Having made no preparations of their own.

When you die
They might play your favorite song
or they might play a more "appropriate" song
as they lead you away
and some people will be scolding themselves
about forgetting where they parked

When you die
They may have forgotten that you didn't
believe in the afterlife

Quotations from Leviticus notwithstanding

When you die
You could be the the one who made
the most important impact on your daughter or son's life
You might have their life worth living

When you die
It may be to no applause

When you die
It may inspire your mother's gynaecologist
to visit a church for the first time in almost half a decade
and feel genuine empathy for the rituals of human dignity
regardless of the tribe

When you die
none of your siblings may attend
the rain might pore on your last parade
and people might go home early

When you die
Everybody may just have a great time
heads beaming, shoulders high

When you die
It might be the longest day of Summer
with waterfights in the park near you were born.

When you die
You will have lived to see
all your ambitions come alive
Even if that penpusher "Reality"
explicitly states otherwise.

WESTLEY BARNES *is an Irish person, living among the British and other curiously confounded international types in Norwich. He teaches burgeoning adolescents how to speak abstractedly about Americans and their fictiveness, and writes poetry and socially aware social media comments when he is distracted from important-sounding bureaucracy. His writing has appeared in The Irish Times, The Bell and the Cáca Milis.*

Blythe Zarozinia Aimson ~ common name: voracious eater of detritus

this catfish eats fascists
in 90 years u will find
skull fragments
crushed jawbone
metallic insignia
in my inflamed intestines
having been too proud to excrete proof
of a justified political murder

this catfish eats Nazis and
bald slimy and smiling i
dissolve military uniform of all ranks
w/o discrimination in stomach acid

this catfish kills fascists
hoping to surpass all other serial killers
in number
  morality
  longevity
a legend in underground anti-fa punk scenes
the fish that killed unnumbered alt-reich arschlochs

this catfish
has eaten and eaten and
eaten flesh that tasted rotten
well before the fucker died
soaked in caustic diarrhoea popularised
by fear w/o statistical evidence or
                         reason or
                         empathy

this catfish acknowledges w/ great sadness
ur unpleasant political standpoint refuses to die
however
unlike ideas a man dies easily and
my appetite for digestively destroying
nazi pond scum is still unsated and
unconfined by a mortal conception of time

this catfish kills and eats and shits fascists

BLYTHE ZAROZINIA AIMSON is currently studying an MA in Poetry at UEA. Blythe thinks lizards are cool. Blythe is a Virgo. Blythe was also a doll so unpopular, it was produced only for one year in 1972

Rosamund O'Donnell ~ Home

They say home is where the heart is.
But - I'm afraid to say - my heart is a little indecisive and
very dispersed.
Sometimes I keep knocking at the wrong door.
Trying to stay in places where I am uninvited.
Through the open curtains I glimpse everything I think I
want inside.
Up turning plant pots and door mats for a spare key until
eventually
I stand on the porch, lean on the door bell and wait.
Sometimes a place is home for a while.
A pit stop home.
A small pocket of joy on a dark road.
I have to take care to notice when I am out staying
welcome.
The conversations stop as you walk in the room.
The glass that stops being filled at the dinner table.
A long silence.
Sometime I give my heart away to an empty house.
The locks have changed.
So I smash a window to climb into a place place filled with
peeling paint and broken door hinges.
Laughing at jokes told by people who are no longer present.
Stoking an empty fireplace as if there were embers.
I curl up and remain here out of habit; because I miss what
was once inside of it.
You should know that I don't trust my heart very often.
It is very easily deceived into thinking it knows what it wants.
Where it should rest.
Home is a place where you are not a stranger.
Walls don't welcome you.
People do.
It is where you are known.
Properly.
Fully.
Expectant for you.
Loved.
You could be in a city of strangers but the moment you
bump into a familiar face well... isn't that Home?
So. Meet me at the airport.
Or a coffee shop.

I might not be entirely there myself. My heart is somewhere
   else waiting to catch up.
But since you are here, I am known.
Since I am no stranger to you:
I am home.

ROSAMUND O'DONNELL *loves Jesus. If you are reading the bios looking for clues as to what her poetry is about - it's probably about Jesus.*

NOVEMBER

Ellen Renton ~ To the British Government on the 3rd of December 2015

Don't make me a war poet.

Don't make me wrap my rhymes
around headlines
and break
each time your censors
mould my words to mistakes.

I don't want my stanzas enlisted in your cause.

You can't conscript each clause
and push it
up the page
until it goes
over the top.

Don't make me a war poet.

Don't define the final flick of my ink.
What gave you the right
to think that my waltzing words
would fall into step
with that heavy footed march,
your killer trigger blink?

I don't want my rhythmic feet booted.

I don't want my verse
dressed in uniform,
nor my T's crossed
with tortured bodies
painted thickly on a makeshift hearse.

Don't make me a war poet.

Can I write with a white feathered quill
and conscientiously object?
If I can,
I will refuse recruitment
and wordlessly watch on

as your death toll collects.

Today it is all ringing true;
the Old Lie in Owen,
the Generals in Sassoon,
and if I should die
I'll think only this of you

if you were ashamed
you did not show it.
You exhaled
with an iambic clap
and condemned my generation
to being war poets.

***ELLEN RENTON** has performed at nights such as Flint and Pitch, Loud Poets, and Inky Fingers, and in venues including the Scottish Parliament and the Leith Theatre. She took part in the spoken word project Words First run by BBC1Xtra and the Roundhouse, and with support from The Nurturing Talent Fund, in September 2016 she released 'Beginnings'; a CD collection combining poetry and music. Her work has been featured by BBC Radio Scotland and Young Scot. An English Literature graduate from the University of Glasgow, she is now studying for an MA in Creative Writing: Poetry at the University of East Anglia.*

N.A. Jackson ~ *Excerpt from* Microeroticon

The small crash of a single drop of rain resounds in the night when each noise is magnified by the hollow dome of the sky. Among the tangled stems of vine and bindweed, deep in a moss-carpeted cleft between two boulders, an eye blinks. Another splash resonates against the crumpled leaves of dock, yet another, until the percussion of drops suffuses into a steady hiss. Rain, seeping into cracks in the baked earth, moistening the parched lips of flowers, slicking the limbs of trees until they sag under the weight of wetness. The eye blinks open, a finger of flesh tipped with a retina and lens, reaching out and recoiling at the touch of each drop, but hungry for the humidity. They stir inside a casing of parchment, looking out and tasting the rivulet of water that floods the garden of moss. The parchment softens to the texture of semolina, then to a milky mucous. The mouth reaching out, extending beyond the limits of last-known things: the dust of this epiphragm, now dissolving. They taste rain, soil, leaf, stone and pools of deliquescence. Life returns to long-dry tissues, blood courses in veins, ducts fill with fresh liquid, sensory organs pulsate and, deep within, a gonad throbs.

Their senses quicken, recognizing the urge: urge to move, to taste, to explore, to find a mate – the sexual urge doppeled. The snail confounds pronouns in the singular - containing he and she - the male and female organs lie folded up beside each other like tiny washing up gloves coiled about with a spaghetti of ducts. Nestled close to the sexual organs, a separate chamber begins its task of preparing a barbed dart, formed of calcareous secretions. Like a murderess with a knife hidden in a velvet reticule plotting treachery.

To stay within the safety of this crevice is decay; to move, to seek, to reach out and risk death, is life. And so, with infinite care, for each contact of their moist mantle with the gritty substrate inflicts pain, they move – twitching, withdrawing, shrinking back but ultimately moving forward, leaving the moss garden and the shelter of the rocky crevice and setting forward on a trail: something has passed here, an otherness. With their lips they sample the chemical trace left behind. A chemical so potent that not even the coursing rain can wash it away.

Oblivious in their search, blinded by the urge, they are unaware of a great flurry of black wings settling and the belligerent glare of an eye, glowing like molten gold. It is death itself, settling down and raising a skewer of sulphur-tinged chitin to stab. At the last moment, with a swift muscular contraction, they withdraw into their carapace. One, two blows fall and glance off, a third, aimed at a weak point in their armour, might have struck home but the blow does not come – death stalks by, distracted by some softer target that wriggles past. They send out a wavering tentacle, moments pass, and then, sensing their luck, they trundle on. The skewer is busy disemboweling the other, less lucky– drawing out a trail of twitching innards.

Hidden in a thicket, the killer's mate is sending out its throbbing call: "*fuck me, fuck me, fuck me; fuck me or feed me, fuck me or feed me; fuck me, fuck me, fuck me*".

N.A. JACKSON *is the author of two collections of short fiction: 'Visits to the Flea Circus', Elastic Press, 2005 and 'The Secret Life of the Panda', Chomu Press, 2011. He has a home in East Anglia where he is perfecting his theory of the impermanence and brevity of life. 'Microeroticon' was published in 'Milk: An Anthology of Eroticism' from Salõ Press.*

Anna Cathenka ~ Moths

I have decided to use moths in this poem as a metaphor for my prevailing sexualities, such as: THE HAWK MOTHS (particularly in terms of behaviour). IE:

> *Death's Head*
> *Convolvulus*
> *Spurge*
> *Bedstraw*
> *Small Elephant*
> *Humming-Bird*

Or in reference specifically to cunnilingus, THE PROMINENT MOTHS (*Swallow Prominent, Lesser Swallow Prominent, Three-Humped Prominent, Great Prominent, Coxcomb Prominent, Scarce Prominent*, etc.)

See also: *Buff-Tip Moth, Chocolate-Tip Moth, Buff Arches Moth*.

And in the depths my *Glaucous Shears*, my *Broad-barred White* teeth, the *Grey Dagger* on your *Splendid Brocade*. Such *Pale Stigma*, my *Black Collar, Flame Shoulder* and *Great Dart*. All gone *Southern Rustic* with underuse. Ah, *True Lover's Knot*!

but beyond base behavioural activity, desire

like how i love men with a sort of *Kentish Glory* / want to be with women as a *Red-Necked Footman*

it is this that makes me masculine, *my Light Crimson Underwing*, i am a *Ghost Swift* in the night, cackling with the camp *Fox Moths*, the *Drinker Moths* – vada that *Lackey Moth*, girls

but with a *Satin Lutestring*. always a but, like *Scarce Silver Lines*, like
but i will become an *Old Lady Moth*, no *Figure of Eighty* for *December Moth*

o me
i would take my sexualities then and retire to the woods

become *Oak Egger*, *Grass Egger*, *Pale Oak Egger*, and eventually

Small Egger, crawl underleaf and remember

    Dark Tussock Moth

    Puss Moth

    Ruby Tiger Moth

ANNA CATHENKA *is the 2017/18, Ink, Sweat & Tears scholar for the MA Poetry at UEA. Her first pamphlet,* Dead Man Walking, *will be published early this year with New Fire Tree Press. Her series* Prayerbook for Tree *was recently released by Smallminded Press. Anna's writing has appeared in* International Times, Stride, The Clearing *and* Partisan Hotel *amongst others. She has performed her collaborative project* Polar Bear Drag Kings *at the Anathema reading series in Bristol and as part of The Enemies Project. Anna can be found online @annacathenka*

Angus Brown ~ I'm igneous

They call him Ozymandias:
With granite face and broken lip,
They say he lost his paramours,
Who sank into the mud.

But legends are not made of stone,
And some of us just want to bone,
Will barely blink, won't even moan
When you tell us we are sluts.

Observe of me, Asmodeus,
Listen Andromalius,
I sing of sidelong Orpheus,
I tell of sodden Sychaeus,
I've diamond thighs; a brow to wipe,
And don't you doubt my wanderlust;
I'm molten, rock-hard, marvellous,
Don't underestimate me;
I'm igneous.

Hence in a shroud I sail Meniscus,
Unheard sometimes, sometimes pretentious,
But always me, and always gorgeous,
Here I come a-rumbling as
Thunder in the night.

Last night I staggered Morpheus,
Scarce nothing left now to discuss,
Than Somnia or phosphorus,
The tension's thick its viscous you could cut it with a knife.

Observe of me, Asmodeus,
Listen Andromalius,
I sing of sidelong Orpheus,
I tell of sodden Sychaeus,
I've diamond thighs; a brow to wipe,
Don't you doubt my wanderlust;
I'm molten, rock-hard, marvellous,
Must I remind you?
I'm igneous.

And you, O lowly listener,
Stalker, viewer, mariner,
Who hears me limning pantheons,
Who comes to me with cheeks a-brazen;
Remember me a-blazing.

Observe of me, Asmodeus,
Listen Andromalius,
I sing of sidelong Orpheus,
I tell of sodden Sychaeus,
I've diamond thighs; a brow to wipe,
Don't you doubt my wanderlust;
I'm molten, rock-hard, marvellous,
Must I say it again?
I'm igneous.

I am invincible,
Unbeatable on electric stage.
Indefatigable: seer, actor, jackal, sage.
I'm shedding off my shackles I've long since divorced stable,
Directed like on cables, in my elemental fables,
I'm hypercharged, I'm amorous,
I'm superwoman, ravenous,
Prometheus, They envy me;
I'm motherfucking igneous.

ANGUS BROWN is a UEA undergraduate reading BA Film Studies and English Literature. He's flattered that you've read all the way to the end of his poem, and would give you a hug in person purely for that. Read more of his nonsense here: https://thedarkandthelovelyblog.wordpress.com

Poppy Rose ~ from a he to a she

From a he, to a she I've been walking,
running away as fast as I can.
Born to be a woman,
cursed with the body of a man.

Nothing could be further from the truth,
than to think I had no reason to cry.
When any mirror on a wall could have told you,
my reflection was no more a lie.

I could give you more than a thousand reasons,
more than I care to say.
Why my waiting has seemed more than a life time,
and a life time that now seems so far away.

I've sat alone in depression,
raised my glass when it's been half full.
Denied myself expression,
more times than I care to recall.

Been scorned for not having a birth right,
laughed at ridiculed and abused.
And by those who should know better,
accused of being confused.

I've jumped through hoops when command,
carried the pain, burned bridges in my wake.
Bargained with lies and bartered with tears,
and often found myself the object of hate.

I've rejected my birth to the disapproval of some,
been outcast by more than a few.
But in all of my time I have never once been unsure,
that who I am cannot be dictated my you.

From a he, to a she I've been walking,
sure footed in the path to my goal.
Never doubting myself for one moment,
when I say I am female from my heart to my soul.

I've never tried to be someone special,
and the tears I have cried are not so too.
Now I've answered all your questions,
so tell me what else do you expect me to do.

This isn't some kind of ambition,
that takes on a life of its own.
So don't say I'm invading your space,
or push me aside demanding I leave you alone.

A snip or two here and a realignment there,
will only stop some of the tears I cry.
And though in myself I'll feel better,
I will still be the same person inside.

I know I will never be happy,
and a mirror will never be my friend.
But my reflection is only skin deep,
and how I feel matters more in the end.

So from the moment they lit my candle,
until the day they blow it out.
I've been and always will be,
a woman beyond any doubt.

POPPY ROSE *says: I am dreamer and a believer in the
goodness of people. In my way and through my poetry and
my life, I like to feel I am a campaigner against all things
hateful. I whole-heartedly believe in our rights to live a life
free from prejudice, hate, fear and persecution. A belief
which I hope you will see reflected within my work.
Whenever possible I enjoy passionately reading my poetry
in public. My poems cover a variety of subjects from hate
through to love.*

Gwen Davis ~ in october, perhaps

it is hard to find words for you.
i can talk about you but
only in statements.
you have grown hazy
though i remember your shape and
the space in between
you and me

(or the lack of it)

you have clawed at my thoughts,
prised them apart,
fit yourself in every crevice.
i am thinking of you now
as i always am.
i am angry but not really with you.
this is my mistake
because i showed you my weakness
and instinct failed me this time.

i am no longer sure i could pick you from a crowd;
passersby take your form
and i live in perpetual fear that you'll find me
or rather i will find you.
i feel the scream
in my head like an infection,
spreading to each function,
necessity,
everyday activity
until there is only the noise we created;
you created

(you forced upon me)

i have erased your particulars
in my effort to erase what you did
but nothing has changed,
you hurt me all the same.

forgive me for your ignorance,
for not calling you out.

i should've been louder,
i should've been clearer,
there is much that i could've done.
did i invite you in here?
did i create you
to use to excuse my mistakes?

'hello friend, it's been a while.
i know i've been useless
but you see
nine months ago
i was
Raped.'

only not that.
that particular arrangement of letters
still deprives me of air.

i am learning.
i am teaching myself to
look you in the eye.
i am moulding my form to enclose you,
to smother you
with everything i have left.
this is my compromise for
it turns out i am unable to disappear
(yet)

i exist.
i continue to exist and
i don't want to surrender.
to you i say:
leave me.
let me be on my own.
i won't allow you here anymore.

GWEN DAVIS spent her early years in Oxford but now resides in Norwich near full time. She spends much of her time not reading and instead collects more books for her shelves. She currently studies English Literature with Creative Writing at UEA and has no idea what she wants to do with her life.

Iona May ~ Awkward Mind

I know I'm lucky to be rich enough to have Dyslexic
I know it's not fair because Stupid can't be exchanged
for anything not even printer ink

so I wouldn't usually mention it but

I think Dyslexic is the reason I find it hard to drive
I think Dyslexic is the reason I can't quite believe the
road will continue beyond the brow of the hill

studies should be done and

when the scientists make me choose between my car
and my Dyslexic
when the scientists remind me I'm fond of her and there
may be unknown benefits

I won't hesitate

IONA MAY is on the Creative Writing MA at UEA. She
explores human foibles in her work, especially her own.

Bryony Leslie Barker ~ Butterflies

I only ever lost my school cardigan once
And it was one of the worst things I have ever done
I wondered what my mother would say
When I went home and I told her that I had made this
  mistake
It made me feel sick
A type of sickness that I never knew how to explain
as I complained to my childminder that my stomach hurt
with fists clenched
my palms threaded with finger nail indents
Torturing myself before my mother ever could
It would be like butterflies
only instead of a flutter of nervousness
the wings of these butterflies would feel like carving knifes
  on the inside of my stomach
scraping away each layer of my skin
making their way out from within
but my mouth remained shut
as if my lips were laced with glue
pink skin chapped and woven in this intricate mesh
that once used to be flesh
my teeth slicing through
The more I tried to chew
Make this scaly stew
thin
The more I tried to swallow
This iridescent sick that my body was rejecting
until at last I said it
skin broken and bleeding
the words now trickling and drooling
crawling down my chin
throwing up on myself instead of neatly in my hands
eyes looking up to be greeted by this stare
these eyes that shattered me
as if my body were made out of porcelain
how beautiful it is to be so delicate
a paper doll
paper thin
crumpled and torn
realizing this
I know now

Why I was scared of you
And why I am scared to him too
This deep rooted
Consciousness
Of my own incompetent-ness
That I still continue to apologize for

BRYONY LESLIE BARKER *says I would have never considered myself a poet, but here I am, my words on a page and I'm still hesitant to call myself one.*

Aliyah Husnah ~ writing you out of my system

it isn't the way you had my weight
beneath your fist
only loosening your grip
with every cry i could not hide;
or how you projected every insecurity
into me like a missile
aimed straight into my chest,
trying your best to suppress
the parts that were too much for you;
trying your best to suppress
every single part of me that grew without you

-- and it isn't the way you'd make me as hollow
as your pupils too big to contain you
while i got high off your eyes
i'd already been made prisoner to;
or how *you'd* claim to be feeling like perfection,
trying harder *every* time just to get the same reflection
to shine from cracked glass.
harder still to find affection from corrosion,
to cut me to pieces, to char me to cinders
to find *your* corpse inside *this* girl
-- oh, darling, no,

--it's in the way every hospital i go past
i still look for you through glass,
searching for solace in that scene of you,
white powder laced like fairy dust shaped like a noose
around your nose collapsing in on itself.
tracking every other heartbeat,
tracking every other way you had me
as addicted to our toxicity
as you were to making me as empty
as your silence made me feel.

it's in how i hear your threats ring
every time i hear hendrix's strings or gilmour sing--
how my mind cant help but think of *you*
-- you in every blues guitar lick
like a taste in my ear of your rhythm
you had me set in sync to,
as if the only thing i was made to fit into was you.

it's in the way you still infiltrate my mind
every time i try to find peace,
the way you keep this war going
with words etched into my brain,
driving me as insane as every gaslight
that lit my way back to you
time and time again.

it's in *every* time i hear those words:
"how could you have stayed so long?"
as if it were me who were wrong
for being held down so i knew
where i belonged, as if it were me
who chose to have my self worth
dragged across dirt
so you could have me begging you
to *just fucking hit me* --
because at least then i could *really* feel hurt
at least then these goods
you damaged from the inside out
would be something they could see.

but mostly,
it's in the way you'll *never* know
that just because you had me,
does *not* mean you saved me
and just because *i* survived you,
does *not* mean you made me.

ALIYAH HUSNAH *exists.*

Sophie Essex ~ Objects of Desire - Her

When I said *I like you this way*:

- acrobat
- architect
- motion

I meant autoerotic, sunday afternoon,
heat. I meant orbital, clenched fists,
our concrete apartment /
accidents & bruised tongue

When I said *I like you this way*
I meant milk lapped,
you begging for what I couldn't,
vulpine & submissive in the only way.
I meant commitment
I meant strawberry red, accented,

vital

What are we waiting for?

SOPHIE ESSEX is a softcore bunny existing in Norwich where she falls in love all too often, obsesses over words like 'otch' 'glacial' 'bubblegum', and promotes her adoration of poetry through Salò Press and regular poetry night Volta. Find her @salopress

Acknowledgements

Volta would not exist without the local community which has included: Cafe Writers; The Live-Lit Lounge; Poetry at Olive's (now Jurnet's); The Salon at the Arts Centre; UEA Live; The Poetry Collective; Gatehouse Press & Lighthouse Magazine; poetry nights at the Rumsey Wells hosted by Sean Wai Keung, Kat Franceska, & Rosie Quattromini. You.

I owe so much to the following individuals for their encouragement & support: Kat Franceska, Andrew Hook, Peter Pegnall, Rosie Quattromini, Coleslaw (Jessica Rhodes), Alex Russell, Sean Wai Keung, Olly Watson, Julia Webb.

VOLTA: AN OBSCURITY OF POETS is an anthology compiling poetry and prose from those that read either as main readers or open-mic at our nights during 2017, whether at The Birdcage, The Bicycle Shop, or at The Arts Centre here in Norwich. Admission fees enabled us to pay our main readers and bring this book into being. Thank you.